NEW ENGLAND

CRESCENT

A LAND FOR ALL SEASONS

As the British Empire grew all over the world, the sons of Old England who went out to spread their version of civilization, and, indeed, England herself, were known as "John Bull."

As the influence of New England spread, her people were called "Yankees." And there's an odd relationship between the two names.

Both the English and the French had their eye on the coast of what the English called North Virginia as far back as the mid-16th century. French explorers had gone as far south as Nantucket, the

A "land for all seasons", New England looks beautiful at any time of the year. The lush greens of spring and summer are replaced by the vibrant reds of fall, and the white of winter.

English as far north as Newfoundland. But neither took the country too seriously until some London businessmen hired Captain John Smith, who had made a name for himself in Virginia, to check out the feasibility of setting up a whaling industry in North Virginia.

Smith wasn't the least bit interested in whales, but he was interested in the countryside. He used the merchants' ships and money to explore it, and when he went back to England, he wrote a book about what he found. The merchants didn't mind, by the way, because he was smart enough to load their ships with a cargo of dried fish, which easily paid for the expedition. Smith's book paid him for his trouble. It was called, simply, "A Description of New England", and it was

A LAND FOR ALL SEASONS

an instant best-seller. It was also the first time anyone had called the place "New England." It was his answer to other colonists who called their settlements such things as "New Spain," "New France" and "New Netherlands."

It was the Dutch in New Netherlands who gave the New Englanders the name "Yankee."

The English who settled on the Northern coast were every bit as thrifty and hard-working as the Dutch and it was only natural that the Dutch would resent

the competition. The English had them surrounded, and had already stopped one Dutch attempt to expand into Delaware, so their resentment was confined to such things as name-calling. One of the things they called them was "Jan Quese," John Cheese. It's what passed for wit in the New Amsterdam colony.

The English never were good at pronouncing foreign words or phrases, so among them, "Jan Quese" became "Yankee," and the name stuck.

Almost from the beginning, New England has been a center for manufacturing, and the shoes and sealing wax and thousands of other things they made had to be sold. So they invented a new American character, the travelling salesman. Men from New England fanned out into all the other colonies selling pots and pans, pins and needles and other staples as well as an occasional luxury to make life in a tough country a little bit easier. They also carried news from one settlement to another, and though they were hard bargainers, they were more than welcome wherever they went. And as they went, they spread the name. They were called Yankee Peddlers.

The name earned its place in history during the years just before the Revolutionary War. By that time, a class society had been built, and young men trying to ease themselves into the upper classes set out to build an image for themselves. They wore clothes that were fashionable in London, spoke with disdain about anything that wasn't European and never, never would eat the kind of food most Americans favored. Instead, they preferred what they thought refined Europeans were enjoying. Their favorite dish was macaroni. Most people didn't take them seriously. And behind their

A heavy sky, laden with snow, glowers over the Vermont landscape **far left top,** *but the sun shines on the picturesque resort of Manchester* **center left,** *which comprises Manchester, Manchester Center and Manchester Depot. The distinctive barns and silos of the northern Vermont farms are a familiar feature of the rural landscape* **left and far left bottom.**

A LAND FOR ALL SEASONS

backs, they called them "Macaroni." Then someone wrote a song about them:

> Yankee Doodle went to town,
> Riding on a pony.
> He stuck a feather in his cap,
> And called it macaroni.

By the time war broke out, every American knew the song and it became their marching music. The Yankee Doodle Dandy, probably a Tory at heart, wound up leading people he surely considered beneath him into a war that would make European style very unfashionable for a long time to come.

But New England's roots are clearly European. After John Smith published his best-seller, dozens of Englishmen went to New England to have a look around, but

for one reason or another none was able to establish a colony.

Meanwhile, Queen Elizabeth established the Anglican Church in England. Most people didn't mind, but some felt her church was much too Roman. A small group of them, from a town called Scrooby, felt so strongly opposed they started up their own church. They called themselves "Puritans" because it was their goal to purify the Church of England.

Some of them felt so strongly opposed to the English church they moved to Amsterdam. But other Englishmen they met there seemed to have fallen under the

influence of the Dutch Reform Church, and that was just as bad, in their opinion. They settled in Leyden, on the Dutch coast, and stayed there for 11 years. Then Holland and Spain began to talk of war and the Puritans decided it was time to move on.

Back in Scrooby, William Bradford and another group of Puritans were thinking about moving, too. He had his eye on America, and negotiated a patent with the Virginia Company to allow him to move his people into their colony. A London merchant offered to finance the trip, in hopes they'd make money for him. And so, in 1620, Bradford's group, joined by the contingent from Leyden, set sail for Virginia with a contract that said they would work for the company store for the next seven years.

There were 35 from Holland and 67 from England, together with some pigs, some chickens and goats. During the two-month voyage, they lived on bacon, salt beef, hardtack, cheese and beer. And they lived under very crowded conditions. That's one reason, some say, why they landed on Cape Cod in Massachusetts and

Top left *Just one of the myriad waterfalls at the southern end of the Franconia Notch. The wooden sugarhouse* **below** *is a common sight in Vermont, and tourists flock to the many antique shops in the area* **right.**

THE EARLY YEARS

not Cape Henry in Virginia. Others say they had intended to wind up in New England all along. They didn't like the contract they had signed, preferring to own their own property. More important, they didn't care much for the merchant who owned them for seven years. The fact is Cape Cod was their first landfall. Their story is that they turned south when they spotted the Cape, but ran into shallow water that threatened their ship. Rather than risk a shipwreck, they said, they pulled into Cape Cod Bay to talk it over. As they pulled into the bay, the ship's crew told them that they were outside the jurisdiction of England in this place and they weren't going to take any more orders from them. It was mutiny, pure and simple.

Since English law didn't apply and the laws of the Virginia colony didn't either, there was nothing for it but to make up some new laws. The men of the company got together and signed a compact among themselves that would be the basis of the law of their new colony. It was called the "Mayflower Compact" after their ship. And though, technically, it wasn't a constitution, it later became the basis of the United States Constitution. With it, they agreed to form their own Government "...unto which we promise all due submission and obedience."

Then they set out to find a place to live. A party of men in a small boat explored the Cape Cod shore from Provincetown, where the Mayflower rode at anchor, and a month later decided Plymouth was the place they were looking for. The big ship followed them, and on the day after Christmas in 1620, the first settlers stepped down onto Plymouth Rock to begin building a town.

Only one Pilgrim died during the crossing, four more died before they actually landed and one child had been born. They weren't as lucky on dry land. During their first winter, about half the original group died. But by spring, when the Mayflower sailed back to England, they had a large common house and several homes built. And with the help of the Indians, who were friendly in this part of the country, they planted crops. They even found time to trade with the Indians

The authentic replica of the Brig Beaver II **right** *is one of the principal exhibits in the Boston Tea Party museum in Boston. The bas-relief* **above** *adorns one of the monuments on Boston Common.*

for furs and cut timber for export to England if another ship happened along.

One did arrive. The schooner Fortune came in the fall with 35 new colonists and sailed away again loaded down with furs and wood to sell back home. Good fortune, indeed. To celebrate, the Indians and settlers got together and had a party. It was a magnificent feast that lasted three days with great good cheer for both red man and white. It was a feast of thanksgiving, and the start of a new American tradition.

But within a few weeks the mood of celebration changed dramatically. Word came back that the ship Fortune had the misfortune to be overtaken by a French pirate and the goods the Pilgrims had worked so hard to gather were on their way to France. No profit there. Then the food started to run out. When they had put away stores for the winter, there were only about 50 mouths to feed. Fortune had brought 35 more.

The Pilgrims had secured freedom from a contract that had bound them to a company store. But they really only traded it for a store of their own. For the first several years everything they grew or made belonged to the colony as a whole.

It wasn't good enough, though, and to increase the food supply, the Pilgrim leaders decided to let every man keep whatever food he grew, but at the same time every man was responsible for feeding his own family. Yankee independence had reared its head. The idea worked, and they were free to worry about other problems.

One of their problems was a nagging doubt about whether God approved of what they were doing. He certainly wasn't making life easy for them. Then one summer a serious drought added to their troubles. If it didn't rain, they surely wouldn't have enough corn to see them through the winter. So they decided to talk to God about it.

They set aside a day during which no one would work, but gather at the common house, instead, to pray for rain. The prayer meeting lasted more than 9 hours, but the sun kept beating down on the roof. The next day it began to rain. It rained the following day, too. And the day after that. It rained so much, the Pilgrim Fathers thought about having another day of prayer so they could see the sun again. Two weeks later, the rain stopped, the sun did come out, and the crops were saved. If ever a people had a Sign, the Pilgrims thought this was it. They never had a day after that they weren't absolutely convinced God was on their side.

But the London merchants weren't. When they heard the Pilgrims had set up shop in Massachusetts, they applied for, and got, a patent to the land around Plymouth. Neither side trusted the other, and finally the Pilgrims bought the merchants out. In the bargain they got all the land east from Narragansett Bay to the tip of Cape Cod and north almost to Boston. They also got a sloop for trading, a fur station in Maine and a fishing station at Cape Ann in Northern Massachusetts.

Most of all, they were delivered from bondage, as they saw it. They owned their own land, and it was legal. Every settler was given an acre in town and 20 acres to farm. A common pasture was established, and everyone had free access to it for grazing their cattle. God, and the London merchants, had spoken.

Concord's magnificent Statehouse is shown **top left.** *The Prentis Rooms* **right** *and the Concord coach* **left** *are exhibited in the capital's museum.* **Far right** *is the Conway Scenic Railway and* **below left** *and* **above** *is the "Old Country Store", one of the first buildings in the area.*

Under the Mayflower Compact, government was relatively simple. They elected their own Governor and other officials and everyone in town participated in the process. But then the colony began to grow. People who were living in Barnstable or Provincetown or even just across the harbor in Duxbury found it hard to get to Plymouth for important meetings. To make it easier for everybody, they sent one person from each town to sit in on the meetings and report back to them in their own town meetings.

Plymouth, almost by accident, got a representational form of Government, and town meetings became a part of the American way of life.

But if the rules William Bradford's colony lived by reflected the opinions of the people who lived under them, not everyone shared the same opinions.

One of them was a young minister named Roger Williams. When he got to Boston in 1631, his first act was to refuse a call to become minister of the church there. It wasn't pure enough for him, he

said. The church at Salem needed a minister, too, and Williams was invited down to be interviewed. John Winthrop, one of the most respected men in the colony, found Williams a little too pure for the Puritans of Salem, so he didn't get the job.

His next stop was Plymouth. They didn't need a minister there, but he was willing to take an assistant's job. They were pretty pure in Plymouth, but it bothered Roger Williams to see that members of the colony who went to England for visits worshipped in the Church of England and nobody back home did anything about it. In addition to accusing them of being "impure," he also began spreading stories that the Massachusetts grant wasn't worth the paper it was written on because it had been drawn up by the King of England, and the land it gave away belonged to the Indians, not the King.

Part of the Massachusetts law required citizens to go to church regularly and to pay taxes to support the church. "You can't do that," said Williams. "Civil Government shouldn't interfere with religion."

The magistrates didn't know whether to brand him a heretic or a lunatic.

Whatever they called him, they had to be careful. He had got the job as minister in Salem, and had a lot of followers there. The magistrates bit their tongues and bided their time. Then he did it. He told his congregation that they should cut themselves off from the other Massachusetts churches and go their own pure way.

THE COAST

The colony's leaders had to act, and they did. Roger Williams went on trial, was found guilty and ordered to be banished from Massachusetts. In effect, they told him if he believed so much that the white man should pay the Indians for the land, go buy some. Roger Williams already had.

He had long since made friends with the Narragansett Indians and had bought a strip of land from them at the head of Narragansett Bay. It was outside the boundaries of Massachusetts, and by going there he fulfilled the sentence of banishment. By spring, others who believed his philosophies joined Williams there, and he had no choice but to establish a colony for them. He laid out a town he called Providence Plantation and laid down a set of laws that made Providence more like the modern de-

mocracies than anything the world had ever seen.

Religious freedom was at the heart of it. In Massachusetts, the government and the church were hopelessly intertwined. Roger Williams untangled the mess for his colony. His law was civil law only. Anybody could go to any church, or to none at all. All men, or at least all

The sea has always played a large part in the lives of New Englanders and even now there are those who earn their living on it, including the lobster fishermen **below.** *The many resorts along the New England coastline offer the visitor a wide range of boating activities, from cruising to deep sea fishing.*

landowners, got together every couple of weeks in town meetings to have their say in making rules they all lived by.

They traded with the Indians and exported to England, they even traded with the Dutch down in New Amsterdam. Roger Williams was a man completely without prejudice. And he became a rich man for it.

Little by little over the next few years other exiles from Massachusetts wandered down the Narragansett Bay and established towns they called Portsmouth, Warwick and Newport.

One of the early arrivals was a strong-minded woman named Anne Hutchinson. Her reputation was established in Boston where she held weekly discussions over afternoon tea about what the Reverend John Cotton was talking about in his sermon the previous Sunday. Cotton, one

of the great clergymen of his time, respected her and heartily approved this extension of the Word. But then Mrs. Hutchinson began adding ideas of her own to the discussions. That won't do, said John Winthrop and the Magistrates. She was put on trial, found guilty of heresy and banished from the colony.

She was taken in by William Coddington, who had already established a new colony at Portsmouth. Later, in 1643, the New England Confederation

Characteristic of the buildings in Maine's smaller settlements are the Sea Grill Restaurant **above right,** decorated with colorful window boxes, and one of the most photographed lighthouses in America, at Pemaquid Point **left. Above** Camden River's waterfalls run below the main street in Camden, and cascade into the harbor.

seemed to be casting greedy eyes on the Narragansett Bay area, to annex it into the Massachusetts colony. The four towns on the bay, never united, decided it was time to stop the threat. They joined forces and sent Roger Williams to London to get a charter to the land from Parliament. It took him a year, but he did it, and in 1647, the four towns joined together and established the colony of Rhode Island. Ironically, Roger Williams, who believed the British had no right to give away New England land, spent a year of his life trying to convince them they should give it to him.

Puritans from Massachusetts went over into Connecticut, too. But in most cases, no magistrates ordered them to go. Within the first ten years of the colony, men went out from Plymouth in search of

trading opportunities. When they heard about it, the Dutch in New Amsterdam staked out a claim on the Connecticut River by setting up a trading post where Hartford is today. That led the English to the spot, and they set up a competing post up-river at Windsor.

The traders went back to Plymouth with tales of the beautiful fertile valley they had found, and America's first westward movement began. The Dutch had claimed the Connecticut River Valley

as their own, but it wasn't long before "John Cheese" and his cousins elbowed the patroons back down to New Amsterdam where they built a wooden wall at the northern end of their settlement and issued a stern warning to Plymouth not to come one step closer than that.

The New England countryside is possibly the most beautiful in all the United States. And of all the countryside in New England, the Connecticut River Valley, even after 350 years of civilization, is absolutely fantastic. In 1635, it must have been like a Garden of Eden.

Word of it had reached London, and a member of the Council for New England, the Earl of Warwick, decided it would make a dandy gift for some of his friends. He gave all the land at the mouth of the river to a group of noblemen, all Puritans, that included Lord Saye, Lord Brooke and Sir Richard Saltonstall. To protect their new interest, they asked John Winthrop, Jr., to go there and build a town before the Dutch came back. Winthrop, in turn, went to Thomas Hooker, pastor of the church at Newtown, across the Charles River from Boston.

Hooker and his flock were alarmed at the way Newtown was growing in 1635. It was getting to be a big city and they didn't like it at all. They should see it today! It's called Cambridge, and it's a Boston suburb. And though everyone agrees it's one of the best parts of one of America's best cities, it undeniably has become big.

But if it was wide open spaces Hooker and his people wanted, there was plenty of that in Connecticut. And so, with Winthrop's help, a band of them went west and settled up and down the river in towns that stretched from Springfield down to Saybrook and then even leaped over Long Island Sound to include two towns at the eastern end of Long Island; Southhold and Southampton. All of it was called Connecticut, and all of it was under a code of laws similar to Rhode Island's with Thomas Hooker as leader.

The Dutch were really getting nervous now. Not only were the English moving down across Connecticut, but they had a foothold on Long Island as well. Then, as if to add insult to injury, a new boatload of Puritans landed in Boston from London. They didn't like Massachusetts much and began looking around for a better place to live. They found it in a place they called New Haven, and, without bothering to ask anyone for permission, moved there in 1637.

They were led by Reverend John Davenport and a former Londoner named Theophilus Eaton, who had much different ideas about government than the Puritans who had preceded them. The Word of God was law enough for them. The Bible didn't say anything about jury trials for instance, so they didn't see any need for them. Yet they thrived as a colony and attracted others who expanded New Haven's influence as far south as Greenwich, at the very doorstep of New Amsterdam.

The Massachusetts Bay colony was sending settlers north into New Hampshire and Maine, too. But there were few firebrands among them, and they were generally content to live under Massachusetts rule. All was well with the world as far as Massachusetts was concerned.

THE COAST

But then the trouble began. As emigrants moved out onto the frontier from Massachusetts, they weren't too careful about whose land they took. The Indians, who had been quite friendly up until that time, didn't like it and took to murdering settlers.

The Puritan leaders took that as a sign from God. If the natives were looking for trouble, they reasoned, it was God's way of telling them they should take Indian land by force. How else to explain this sudden change in Indian attitude?

They sent out a force of soldiers into Connecticut to bring the red man to his knees. The soldiers found an Indian village where a council of war was taking place and, as a result, every Indian from miles around was there. Surely another of God's signs, they said. So they surrounded the village, killed all the Indians and burned it to the ground. It removed a lot of menacing Indians from the scene, and it also freed a lot more land for settlement.

The war was over quickly, and the Indian "problem" was removed, for all practical purposes, forever. But it made them realize that they all faced common problems and the best way to solve them was through a united front. Every colony had lustful eyes on the lands around Narragansett Bay, and every Puritan in every other part of New England despised the liberal government of Rhode Island. That convinced them they should combine their resources if they ever expected to rid the world of red men and liberals.

And so, in 1643, leaders from Massachusetts, New Haven, Connecticut and Plymouth sat down together in Boston and drafted an agreement that would give each of them the other's "…advice and succor upon all just occasions." When they heard about it, people in Maine and Rhode Island asked if they could be included in the agreement, too. Rhode Island, obviously, was out of the question. That was one of the problems the rest of them thought they needed to unite against. And as for Maine, they had welcomed political exiles from Massachusetts as well as voicing occasional opinions in favor of letting everyone in the colony have a voice in government.

On the grounds of their extreme radicalism, therefore, Maine and Rhode Island weren't allowed to be parties to this new alliance they called The New England Confederation.

If the Puritan leaders were intolerant of other people's ideas, they had some good ideas of their own, and this Confederation was one of them. It was the first time any North American colonies were joined together, yet the agreement recognized that each of them was fully independent of each other and of England. It provided for common protection, with the cost of arms to be

The Portland Lighthouse **right** *can be seen from the rugged coastline of Port Elizabeth* **far right bottom** *on a clear day. Maine is noted for its beautiful, still lakes and forests* **center right** *and picturesque harbor towns* **top right.** *Fort Edgecomb* **above** *in Acadia National Park, is a remnant of the 1812 war.*

shared by all of them. It had provision for the extradition of escaped prisoners and slaves among the colonies. And only the group as a whole could declare war or negotiate treaties. It would be another century-and-a-half before there would be a United States. But in 1643, they were well on their way.

The Massachusetts Bay Colony was, by that time, first among equals. It had been established a few years after the Pilgrims arrived at Plymouth. The first

THE COAST

settlers were considerably different from the dour Puritans; they were lusty Elizabethans. On Mayday in 1627, they built an 80-foot maypole topped with deer antlers and, as William Bradford later wrote, the fun included "...drinking and dancing aboute it for many days togeather, inviting the Indean women for their consorts, dancing and frisking togeather like so many faeries, and worse practices."

Well! That couldn't last. And it didn't, not for much more than another year. Finally, charging that the rowdies had sold guns to the Indians, the Governor of Plymouth dispatched Captain Miles Standish to run them out of the country. Fortunately, as Standish himself later admitted, most of them were drunk when the attack took place, and it was fairly easy to send them packing.

And before they could come back from England, other Englishmen, of more gentile Puritan persuasion, moved in, chopped down the maypole and made Massachusetts Bay safe for God-fearing people.

They changed the name of the little town from Merriemount to Braintree, and very quickly established another settlement at Weymouth. Then a new breed of Puritans began arriving. People like Roger Conant and Reverend John White who agreed that the Anglican Church needed purification, but their idea was to stay with the Church and save it from itself. They got permission to establish a New England colony on the basis of the good fishing there. And naturally, they believed Puritans would make the best fishermen.

The company they formed, the Massachusetts Bay Company, was both chartered and headquartered in England as were all the trading companies that ruled the colonies in America. But this one was different. It made the New World seem so attractive, the directors of the company decided to go there themselves. That meant the company's headquarters would have to be moved. Nothing like that had ever happened before.

Most of the influential Puritans had, until that time, been forced to stay in England to be certain their American interests were protected. But most of them were as shocked by the moral atmosphere there as William Bradford had been by the Merriemount maypole in America. They were convinced God was about to come down on England with a vengeance, and they didn't want to be there when it happened.

The popular summer resort of Kennebunkport **right** *attracts artists and writers, and contains one of the best play-houses in the area. The Boon Island Boat Races are also held here. Providence, the state capital of Rhode Island, has some lovely old buildings, like the church* **above.**

Moving the whole Massachusetts Bay Company to Massachusetts Bay made perfect sense.

Among the Puritans who moved with it was John Winthrop, Lord of Groton Manor. As governor of the company, it was his decision to move it, and once they got to Massachusetts, it would have to be his decision where to locate his headquarters. Salem was well-established when he arrived, but most of its citizens lived in tents or worse, and the last thing they needed was more settlers. He moved down the bay and picked a spot to build a settlement which they called Charlestown. Before long, other towns were established in the same area, including one across the river called Boston.

Within a decade, the colonies on the bay had attracted 20,000 people from England and building houses for them and

RHODE ISLAND

selling them food became a major industry. What was left over they exported to other American colonies where they traded for local products which, in turn, were exported to England. John Winthrop and his people became the merchant princes of the New World. And that made them not only rich, but influential as well.

Nothing succeeds like success, of course, and more and more people flocked into the bay area from the Old Country.

Rhode Island is the smallest state in the United States of America but contains a variety of attractions. A downtown view of Providence is shown **right,** *with the County Court House* **below.** *Pumpkins ripen on a lawn* **opposite page top right.**

The more there were, the better for business and the greater the need for whole new towns. The government was liberal in giving land for towns, and since a great many of them were established at around the same time, most of the old New England towns follow the same pattern.

They began with a big square in the center, sometimes as much as six or seven acres, which they called a "common." It was a public park, a parade ground, the center of activity. At the most command-ing spot along the common they built a church, and right next door, an elegant house for the minister. Another building

lot was earmarked for a school. The remaining land around the common was divided into lots for houses, with the best going to the leaders and then to the original settlers. Anything left over was held to be sold to new settlers. Some land was held for expansion just beyond the common, but clearly, the best homesites in any town were right on it. Though the

RHODE ISLAND

building lots were generous, each resident also got a patch of farmland outside town. And every town included a tract of land for a common pasture and a section of woodland free to all for cutting firewood.

They named their towns after places they had left behind in England and their society was built along ideas they had brought with them. But there was an important difference in New England. They still believed in a class structure, but believed just as strongly in the idea that if you worked hard enough you could rise above class and become as important as any man. It was an idea that made a great

Newport, at the southern end of Rhode Island, still retains an appealing colonial seaport appearance. The city is renowned for its America's Cup Races and music Festivals, magnificent mansions and restored 18th and 19th century commercial shops that line historic Bowden's Wharf.

THE PAST PRESERVED

many of them rich as well as important.

. The colonial towns are the ones the travel folders so often describe as "typical New England." "Typically" New England is probably a better description because they weren't planned towns in the modern sense, and the plan didn't find wide acceptance in other colonies. It's not an easily expandable town design; late arrivals who don't get to live around the common wind up with a feeling of being on the outside looking in. Yet, it's a comfortable way to live and the towns that kept their original character are a joy to visit.

But what today's visitor sees as typical of New England are the industrial towns like Chicopee or Waltham in Massachusetts. The first of them was Waltham, built in 1813. It was the model for dozens of New England towns from Lawrence and Lowell in Massachusetts to Manchester and Nashua in New Hampshire. And all of them were built to the specifications of the boards of directors of companies located in Boston.

The towns themselves were designed like factories, with houses, churches and stores put in precise locations with no thought given to their relationship to each other. In some places, like Springfield and Waltham, a town already existed when the factory builders arrived. But many were built from scratch to be near the water power that was so important to a successful factory.

It all began in 1812 when Francis Lowell of Boston took a trip to Europe and was impressed by work the British were doing with power looms. Cotton was plentiful in the South, free energy was plentiful in New England and waves of immigration were beginning to assure a good, and inexpensive, labor pool. It wasn't long before the Cabots of Boston decided to get into the business, and the competition made it all an even more exciting proposition.

In fact, the annual report of one of the companies a few years later told stockholders, "The rumor of your profits will make people delirious!"

The towns they built are a valuable clue to why that was so. They built housing, often tenements, for the workers,

and leased them to boarding house operators. The mill owners fixed the amount to be charged, and decided which house a new employee should live in. The cost of the room and board was deducted from monthly paychecks. The operators

of the housing were controlled by the owners, and were held directly responsible for any improper conduct or violations of the rigid ten o'clock curfew. They were also charged with making sure the workers went to church every Sunday.

Once a candy peddler accidentally wandered into Chicopee and was quickly run out of town because it was considered unseemly for working people to spend their money on anything so frivolous. The workers were mainly women who worked from five in the morning until after seven in the evening. They got a half-hour off for lunch and another half-hour for dinner. Then it was home to a room that may have been shared by six girls. In the little time they had before

Formerly the homes of wealthy colonial merchants, Newport contains many splendid mansions: the Breakers **top left;** *the Elms* **below right;** *Rosecliffe* **left;** *and Marble House* **below** *and* **above right.**

bedtime, there were culturally-uplifting activities like lectures and poetry readings. But as the Civil War approached, they found their cultural uplift in the movement to abolish slavery.

Small wonder!

Not every company town was unpleasant, and in many cases Boston companies actually improved existing towns. It happened in Manchester, New Hampshire. Manchester was run by a huge cotton manufacturer for more than 100 years. Nothing important happened there unless the company agreed it was important. But at the beginning, the company had laid out a handsome city, indeed. It had a broad main street with a row of trees in the center and sidewalks twelve feet wide. It had five public squares, a cemetery and plenty of room for schools. It had sewers, too, and even a "house of correction." The factory itself ran for a mile and a half on both sides of the Merrimac River.

As the business grew, so did Manchester, out-producing the English city that gave it its name and becoming one of the most important cities in the United States. Then the bottom fell out on Wall Street in 1929, and not long after, the bottom fell out in Manchester, too. The factory shut down and more than half the people in town were out of work.

Slowly it grew back, of course, and

today more than 100 companies fill the buildings that were once the mills.

The New England mill towns are duplicated as far west as Indiana, and many can tell the same story as

Manchester. The story has been duplicated hundreds of times in New England itself.

New Englanders have done more than simply export products and ideas to the rest of the country. One of them, Rufus Putnam of Rutland, Massachusetts, exported himself and a group of his neighbors to the Wild West in 1788 and founded the state of Ohio. Years after they first settled in Marietta and helped open the door to later expansion in the West, a bronze tablet was put next to the door of his old homestead in Rutland. It said, in part, "...to him, under God, it is owing that the great Northwest Territory was dedicated forever to Freedom, Education and Religion, and that the United States of America is not now a great slaveholding empire." The plaque was put there in 1898, back in the days when they gave credit where credit was due!

Rufus Putnam knew where he was going when he headed west. A lot of New Englanders didn't. At about the same time, a contingent headed out from Connecticut until they found a valley that looked

inviting. They built a little town around a fort and settled down to raise some corn, thinking of themselves as the most western residents of the whole territory of Connecticut.

Meanwhile, another little group out from Philadelphia found the same valley. "What are you doing in Pennsylvania?" they asked. "It's Connecticut," was the answer. With no oil companies, there were no good maps, so there was no other way to settle the thing than to go to war. It took three wars to dislodge the Yankees from William Penn's territory, and some never did leave. King's grants were at the heart of the problem. The Connecticut grant had no western boundary; Pennsylvania ran as far north as anyone cared to

The capital of Connecticut is Hartford—its lights are seen here reflected in the waters of the Connecticut River **opposite page top.** *Probably the state's most famous institution is Yale University, founded in 1701. Ivy-clad walls lend an air of history to the University's lovely old buildings* **left** *and* **above.**

YALE

say it did. The king was in England, after all. What did he know?

Ah, England! It was inevitable that some day someone would decide it was time to go it alone. And it was just as inevitable that it would be decided in New England.

Westward expansion was one of the reasons. New Englanders were looking west, and so were British businessmen. There was money to be made there and neither wanted the other to have it. Then there was another economic matter, taxes. "Why should Americans pay taxes to England?" they asked. And, more important, why pay to house a British army that nobody asked for in the first place. "This isn't Ireland," they said, "and it's about time somebody did something about it."

Then the British did something they never should have done. It had to do with tea.

Even 150 years after Plymouth, just about everybody in New England had come from some part of the British Isles. And they did like their cup of tea. By 1773, they had found new sources for it, and were buying tea from just about anybody who had it to sell, except the giant British East India Company. London had put a tax on British tea, and that made it more expensive. Besides, the Yankees resented English taxes anyway.

To keep the Company from going bankrupt, Parliament agreed to lower the tax and make British tea competitive in America. American businessmen didn't like that very much and appealed to pamphleteers, who were already quite active against the Mother Country, to stir up public opinion against this outrage.

They did their job and when the British ships arrived in Boston loaded with tea, demonstrators on the docks appealed to the authorities to send them back. But they refused, and so on the night of December 16, 1773, a group of men who looked very much like Indians, but probably weren't, boarded the ships and tossed £15,000 worth of tea overboard.

Parliament wasn't too happy about that. They passed a series of new laws, which became known in New England as "intolerable acts." The first closed the port

of Boston completely until the tea had been paid for. The second said that British officials who were charged with offenses in the line of duty could be sent back to England for trial. And the third called for sending more British troops to America to be housed at Colonial expense.

Yale's graceful old buildings bask in the New England sunshine **left,** *while students study in the splendid library* **above.**

They passed more laws later that changed the basic structure of the Massachusetts Government. Altogether it served to rally more and more New Englanders to the idea of separation from England. And the idea spread down the coast to other colonies as well. In Virginia, where the Assembly set aside a day of fasting and prayer for New England's trouble, Thomas Jefferson sent a message to the other colonies that they should unite in a common front against British oppression. And the other colonies sent food and other supplies to help the people of Boston.

No one sent any money to pay for the tea.

By September, 1774, the plight of Boston had turned public opinion far enough away from England for leaders from every colony, including Samuel Adams and John Adams of Massachusetts and Roger Sherman of Connecticut, to get together in what they called a Continental Congress to decide what to do about it.

What they decided was to stand up for their rights. The right to have a say over their own lives. The right to tax and

PAGEANTRY

govern themselves. The right to protect themselves. The right to all the rights of free subjects of the King.

They considered themselves British subjects and were careful to make that a part of the document they signed. But not careful enough. Their declaration became an issue in the next Parliamentary election, and the voters there came down foursquare on the side of getting tough with America.

Part of the "get tough" policy was yet another law. This one forbidding any New England colony from trading with any foreign country except England or the British West Indies.

The result was more anti-British pamphlets, more muttering on village greens and a new act of protest: local committees buying and storing guns and ammunition. Two committee leaders, John Hancock and Samuel Adams, were considered the biggest troublemakers of all, and orders were sent to General Gage,

the British commander in Massachusetts, to arrest them both and send them back to England for trial.

They might have succeeded, but for a man named Paul Revere. Some years later, in his description of the event, the New England poet, Henry Wadsworth

Longfellow, set the date of Paul Revere's ride as "...the 18th of April in '75." "Hardly a man is now alive," he said, "Who remembers that famous day and year." Even fewer remember these days. The ride and the events that followed it are commemorated by a public holiday in Massachusetts. It's called "Patriot's Day," and it's celebrated on the 3rd Monday in April. Some years it actually falls on the 18th.

The Colonials knew the British were after Hancock and Adams. But the troops charged with the job were in Boston and nobody knew whether they'd go by land or sea to get to Lexington, where their intended prisoners were. Paul Revere agreed to signal the militia with lanterns in the steeple of Boston's Old North Church. Then, after deputizing a friend to light the lights, he rowed across the river to Charlestown. By the time he got there, the signal had been given, so he borrowed a horse and raced off to Lexington. He

then headed on to Concord, where the guns and ammunition were stored, to mobilize the people there.

Early in the morning, the British arrived in Lexington. Paul Revere was there, and later recorded what happened next:

"...We passed through the militia," he wrote. "There were about fifty. When we had got about one-hundred yards from the meeting-house, the British troops appeared on both sides of it. In their front was an officer on horseback. They made a short halt; when I saw and heard a gun fired, which appeared to be a pistol. Then I could distinguish two guns, and then a continual roar of musquetry."

Three weeks later, another Continental Congress declared war on Great Britain.

Lexington and Concord had united the 13 colonies. Down in Virginia, George Washington announced it meant either war or slavery, and made it clear he preferred the former. In London, King

stopped in Medford on the way to awaken and warn the Captain of the Minutemen that the British were coming, then stopped at every house along the way to spread the alarm.

He reached Lexington and warned Adams and Hancock in plenty of time,

Scenes from the exciting New Haven Parade are shown **on these pages** *–colorful costumes, uniforms, flags and banners make for a thrilling display of pageantry and patriotism.*

George III told Parliament he intended to hire foreign mercenaries to deal with the American problem. To Americans, who were still Englishmen at heart, this was a signal that the King was treating them as foreigners. It was an insult they couldn't forgive.

THE PAST RELIVED

The following year, in Philadelphia, the Americans issued a Declaration of Independence that effectively severed any ties with England and its King. From that day, July 4, 1776, they were no longer British colonies, but a new country, The United States of America.

Interestingly, Thomas Jefferson's original draft of the Declaration included the line, '...we must endeavor to forget our former love of them...we might have been a free and great people together." It was removed during the debate that preceded the signing of the document. But it represented the feelings of a great many citizens of New England and the other colonies as well.

After Lexington and Concord, the American "Army," such as it was, managed to surround Boston with the British troops inside. They held it from Breed's Hill in Charlestown. General Gage decided to take the hill away from them by attacking it head-on. His troops were in for a surprise. As they marched toward the hill nothing happened. They got closer and closer. Still nothing. Then, when they were at point-blank range, the Americans opened up on them. About a third of the British were killed before the Americans ran out of ammunition and withdrew.

Soon after, George Washington, now Commander-In-Chief of the American troops, arrived and took command. He set up shop on the south side of Boston, and it wasn't long before the British decided Boston wasn't worth the trouble and moved out. They moved on to New York, with General Washington on their heels.

The war spread to other parts of New England, too. Ethan Allen, from Vermont, and Benedict Arnold, from Connecticut, took over the British forts at Ticonderoga, Crown Point and Fort St. John. And up in Maine, the British burned down the town of Falmouth. But the war didn't get really serious until after the Declaration of Independence had been signed.

One of the British strategies was to cut New England off from the rest of the country. They had a large force in Canada and controlled New York. All that was needed was to retake Boston and connect the two. But they hadn't counted on the

rough country in Vermont and New Hampshire, nor on the determination of the people there to keep them from passing through. General Burgoyne, in his march south from Ticonderoga, found out how determined they were, and by the time he reached Saratoga, in New York, and found regular troops waiting for him, he'd had enough. He surrendered his army of 5,000 men. That ruined the great plan of cutting New England off, and at the same time ruined British morale. More important, it also gave France an excuse to mix into the war. And that tipped the balance.

The Revolution was virtually over in New England at that point, having moved south. It finally ended at Yorktown, Virginia, on October 19, 1781.

America was free to go her own way. And New England was ready and able to show her the way.

Puritanism had attracted a great many business people in England, and poor business conditions there encouraged more and more of them to go to Massachusetts. When they arrived, they had money in their pockets, unlike settlers in other colonies. They had skills, too, and used their money and their skill to set up shop in the new world. Many had been aristocrats, and brought an attitude that made anything but success unthinkable. And, as Puritans, all of them believed hard work was the only foundation of any good life.

Plymouth Rock Memorial **opposite page center,** *protected by a granite portico, commemorates the landing place of the Pilgrims who, after disembarking in December 1620, founded the first permanent settlement north of Virginia. In a tranquil, pastoral setting, the picturesque rural scenes of Old Sturbridge Village* **other pictures these pages** *recreate a New England farming community of the late 18th and early 19th century period. The cottage industries and farm work recreated at the village are dependent upon the same sources of energy as those tapped by the early New Englanders, ensuring the authenticity of the village.*

The result was that long before the war, New Englanders were the business leaders of the entire country. In a country that believed to its soul it had no aristocracy, the Dudleys and Downings, Winthrops and Saltonstalls were behaving as much like aristocrats as any families in England.

By 1640, they were selling codfish to Spain, wooden barrels to the West Indies and beef to anyone who could afford it. Their exports went around the world in ships built in New England, and the ships came back loaded with everything from wine to iron that could be sold in the other colonies.

By 1700, New England traders were doing a thriving business in all parts of the world. Then one of them landed on the coast of Africa, and discovered what British traders knew: The real fortunes were being made in the slave trade. Within a few years, Boston became one of the biggest rum producers in the world and Newport became a boom town as the major port for slave ships. It was a simple economic proposition. Ships from Newport, loaded with Boston rum, went to Africa, traded the rum for slaves and headed for the West Indies. They sold the slaves there, loaded their ships with sugar and headed back to Boston where they sold the sugar to make more rum. Then they went back to Newport to count their money.

Not everyone in New England was engaged in the slave trade, of course, and they respected hard work too much to own them themselves. But the trade made New England prosperous, and that was important to everybody from shoemakers to farmers.

What was most important of all was that anybody at all could, in one way or another, with diligence and thrift, and sobriety, of course, make something of himself. John Hancock's family was a good example of it. Nathaniel Hancock was the first of them to arrive from England. He was a shoemaker, and established a small business in Cambridge. It was nothing big, but big enough to support his 13 children and successful enough to put one of his sons through Harvard. The son, John, became a

THE SLEEPING LAND

The gently rolling countryside of Massachusetts is transformed by a carpet of white, glistening snow **left, above left and above,** *while Chatham Lighthouse* **right** *warns seafarers of the Cape Cod coastline.*

preacher and went to Lexington. His son, Thomas, was born there. Thomas decided he wanted to be a businessman and went to Boston to work in a book store, and before too long established himself as an exporter. He made enough to build a fine house on Beacon Hill, and even sent to England to have a family coat of arms cut in silver and mounted on ivory. His nephew, John, inherited the business and built it even bigger. As the head of one of Boston's leading families, people listened when John Hancock talked about patriotism.

But of all the virtues they admired, education was one of the most important. The Puritans believed the only way to salvation was in the ability to read the Scriptures, and the establishment of schools was as important as churches. Every town had one of each, even poor children learned to read and write. In 1635, the people of Boston established a school along the lines of the English grammar schools they had all attended

themselves. Other towns used the Boston Latin School as the model for their own. The people all shared the cost of the schoolmaster and materials.

In 1647, it became the law in Massachusetts that every town with 50 or more families had to have a school and hire a schoolmaster "to teach all such children as shall resort to him to read and write." The reason for the law was explained in the law itself. "That old

deluder, Satan," it said "wants to keep men from the knowledge of Scriptures by keeping them in an unknown tongue." The word "men" is important there. The schools were established for boys only. There were some private schools for girls, however, and many of them learned to read at home.

They knew from the beginning that reading and writing and vocational training weren't quite enough. As an early historian explained it:

"After God had carried us safe to New England and we had builded our houses, provided necessaries for our livelihood, reared convenient places for God's worship, and settled the civil government, one of the next things we looked for and longed for was to advance learning and perpetuate it to posterity, dreading to leave an illiterate ministry to our churches when our present ministers shall lie in the dust. And as we are thinking and consulting how to effect this great work, it pleased God to stir up the heart of one Mr. Harvard to give one-half of his estate (it being in all about £1,700) towards the erecting of a college, and all his library. After him, another gave £300, others after them cast in more, and the public hand of the state added the rest. The

BOSTON

college was by common consent appointed to be at Cambridge (a place very pleasant and accomodate) and is called (according to the name of the first founder) Harvard College."

Harvard was founded on the traditions of the colleges in England, but added new ideas, particularly in science, that were becoming accepted at the time. By 1650, a little more than 10 years after its founding, Harvard was attracting students from England. Puritan families there sent their sons to take advantage of the environment which was "purer" in Cambridge, Massachusetts, than in Cambridge, England. The college also had two Indian students. The colonists were sure that the savages would be much less savage if they were educated. They gave up the idea later, and settled the Indian problem in a different way.

In a report on the graduates between 1673 and 1707, it was found: "52 came from the Connecticut Colony, eight from New Hampshire, 17 from the Plymouth Colony and but one from Rhode Island. The remainder were from Massachusetts Bay." Three hundred and sixty students graduated from Harvard during the period, and the idea of higher education in America was well-established. But Harvard wasn't highly-thought of in every quarter. As a Boston preacher put it in a sermon:

"Places of learning should not be places of riot or pride. Ways of profuseness and prodigality in such a society lay a foundation of great sorrow. Fond and proud parents should not be suffered to introduce evil customs. 'Tis not worth the while for persons to be sent to college to compliment men and court women. They should be sent thither to prepare them for public service, and had need to be under the oversight of wise and holy men."

What they proposed was a new college, holier than Harvard. In 1701, a charter was issued and the Collegiate School established in Saybrook,

*The twinkling skyline of Boston **right,** seen here from Longfellow Bridge, rises from a soft white blanket of snow into the pink evening.*

BOSTON

Connecticut. Cotton Mather, one of Massachusetts' leaders, was one of the prime movers in the new venture. He had dreamed of being named president of Harvard, but it was a dream Harvard didn't share. Mather knew an opportunity when he saw one, and the Collegiate School, clearly, was it.

But it wasn't big enough. Mather set out to overcome that problem by writing a letter to a former New Englander who had made a fortune and gone back home to England. "Send us money for our new college," said Mather, "and we'll give it your name." But the former Yankee sent other things instead. He sent a box of books, a portrait of the King and some bales of Indian goods, but no money. So Cotton Mather had a garage sale. The stuff brought £300. They used the money to move the school from Saybrook to New Haven and then they renamed it

Modern hotels and office blocks and stream-lined highways and bridges **these pages** are very much a part of Boston, state capital of Massachusetts, but Bostonians find the time to stop a while in one of the many parks—to paint, or to make friends. The Charles River and Boston Harbor provide an idyllic setting for countless pleasure craft of all kinds.

for the merchant who had sent them a picture of the King, Elihu Yale.

More conservative than Harvard, Yale was much more attractive as a school for preachers and for anyone else who admired the "steady habits of Connecticut."

An early President of Yale explained why he thought his was the better of the two schools:

"The greatest disadvantage under which Harvard labours is the proximity of Boston. The allurements of this metropolis have often become too powerfully seductive to be resisted by the gay, and sometimes even by the grave, youths who assemble there for their education. Since the erection of the West Boston bridge, the distance between the towns of Boston and Cambridge is reduced from five to little more than three miles. This fact, as I have been informed by the Governors of the University, has rendered the evil alluded to still greater. The bustle and splendour of a large commercial town are necessarily hostile to study. Theatres, particularly, can scarcely fail of fascinating the mind at so early a period of life."

For all its evils, Boston had more bookstores than any other city in the United States. By 1724 there were enough to form the first trade association for booksellers. In 1700, there were 20 of them in Boston, compared to four in New York. They imported books from England and reprinted some themselves. Before long, they were writing them in New England, too.

Probably the first was William Bradford's "A Relation or Journal of the Beginning and Proceeding of the English Plantation Settled at Plymouth in New England." That mouthful was followed a few years later by another description of New England with a much catchier title: William Wood's "New England Prospect." It became a best-seller in England because of its description of such things as hummingbirds, which the English had not seen before. He also wrote that he spotted a lion at Cape Ann, "not above six leagues from Boston."

Others like John Winthrop and Cotton Mather kept journals which were published later. Mather's was a history of

BOSTON

the church in New England, which, to him, was the same thing as a history of the colony.

The early colonists wrote poetry, too. In 1640, a committee of ministers got together and wrote literal versions of the Psalms so their congregations could sing them in church. It was the first book printed in America, and "The Bay Book of Psalms," as it was called, was a huge success. It was 20 years before the colonies saw another best-seller like it, and that, too, was a book of poetry, Michael Wigglesworth's "Day of Doom." Its verses gave the faithful a grim picture of what could happen to them if they should

stray from the straight and narrow path to salvation. And for a century after, children were required to memorize its verses.

Probably the best-known of the colonial writers was Benjamin Franklin, and his "Autobiography" was the first really important book of colonial America. Though he earned his reputation down in Philadelphia, where many of the people could only read German, Franklin was a New Englander, too. He was born on Milk Street in Boston. He began his career, and educated himself, in a Boston print shop. All he knew he learned from reading, and although both Harvard and Yale as well as

The Ladies Auxiliary to the Veterans of the Foreign Wars of the U.S. **left** *demonstrate their allegiance and loyalty at the Soldiers and Sailors Monument* **far left.** *Much of the original Boston has been preserved, like the Union Oyster House* **below right,** *the oldest restaurant in the city, the Old State House* **below,** *with its distinctive tower, and Beacon Hill* **bottom and bottom left,** *now a National Landmark*

Oxford and Edinburgh University gave him honorary degrees, he never had a formal education.

But for anyone with an interest, there was plenty to read. Shakespeare, Bacon, Spenser and others had already added to England's greatness. And controversy in England during the early years of the Massachusetts Colony produced such diverse literature as Samuel Pepy's "Diary," John Milton's "Paradise Lost," and John Bunyan's "Pilgrim's Progress."

Boston was ready to take her place as one of the world's great intellectual centers after the war, and by the beginning of the 19th century. Samuel Adams had called it the "Christian Sparta," the people were all well-off, if not super-rich, and God was, after all, firmly on their side. They were still rich in what later became known as "the Protestant Ethic." Indeed the first Mayor of Boston didn't mind telling anyone who would listen that the only rule in his home was: "Ask no man to do for you anything that you are not willing to do for yourself." Another New Englander, President John F. Kennedy, was to paraphrase that rule and recommend it to the entire country some 200 years later.

Little by little though, the fire and brimstone had gone out of their religion. Yankee traders travelled a lot, and compared to things they saw in the Mediterranean, in the South Seas and even in other American colonies, even the backsliders among them seemed more than decent. They were by no means ready to pack in their religious beliefs, but they were considerably more liberal than their fathers had been.

As if to demonstrate to the world that New England was changing, the city fathers redesigned the city of Boston. The new style was more delicate than the Georgian buildings they replaced and the scale of the city more graceful and human. Among the new buildings was the 1807 Boston Athenaeum, stocked with several thousand books imported from Paris and London. The Handel and Haydn Society followed it in a few more years, and the message was clear. This was where the new country's intellectual future would be established.

They even began to publish a magazine. "The Monthly Anthology" published the work of such up-and-coming writers as Daniel Webster, a Portsmouth lawyer. It was financed by William Tudor, who had built a fortune shipping New England ice all over the world after having first sold the world on the idea that drinks taste better "on the rocks."

Then, in 1837, a young man named Ralph Waldo Emerson made an address at Harvard that set the tone for the whole

BOSTON

country for a generation and more. Individualism was his Gospel, and nothing suited the American character quite like it. He had been influenced by the Romantic Movement in England, by the calls for personal freedom in the work of Byron and Shelley. He adapted it to the American dream, and gave the world a new "American" to deal with.

Henry David Thoreau and Nathaniel Hawthorne, and in later years John Greenleaf Whittier and other New England writers, searched for a perfect life in much the same way and their ideas went West with the pioneers, a great many New Englanders among them, who built the country.

A few of the great New England writers like Longfellow and James Russell Lowell didn't exactly share Emerson's belief that all men were equal and free to control their own destiny. Their ideas came from Europe, too, but they believed family connections stood for something and they thought money probably helped.

Although New England writers dominated the 19th century, other parts of the country were producing a new American literature, too. James Fenimore Cooper and Edgar Allan Poe were making huge contributions, and Washington Irving of New York was making it fashionable to read books about Americans by Americans. But, beginning with William Cullen Bryant, a newspaper editor from a small town in the Berkshires, Yankee writers began to leave home to find new worlds to conquer. And they took along some of Emerson's ideas that a successful man needed to know the aspects of nature, the thinking of the past and the life of the present.

But if their pens were mighty, New Englanders found other ways to influence the new country. One writer, a newspaperman from Bethel, Connecticut, found a better way after having served 60 days in jail for libelling a prominent churchman. On December 12, 1832, he was released from jail and wrote this description of the event for his paper:

"P.T. Barnum and the band of music took their seats in a coach drawn by six horses which had been prepared for the occasion. The coach was preceded by 40

The city contains many beautiful churches; the exquisite interior of Trinity Church is shown **left,** *its delicate stained glass windows ablaze with vibrant color, while* **below right** *the Old South Church is filled with rich, mellow wooden pews. The magnificent State House, designed by Charles Bulfinch in 1795, features the marble-floored Memorial Hall* **below,** *and* **right** *is the House of Representatives, where above the carved mahogany walls paintings detail events in the history of Massachusetts.*

horsemen, and a marshall, bearing the national standard. Immediately in the rear of the coach was the carriage of the Orator and the President of the day, followed by the Committee of Arrangements and 60 carriages of citizens, which joined in escorting the editor to his home.

"When the procession commenced its march amidst the roar of cannon, three cheers were given by the several hundred citizens who did not join the procession. The band of music continued to play a variety of national airs until their arrival in Bethel (a distance of some three miles) when they struck up the beautiful and appropriate tune of 'Home Sweet Home!' …The utmost harmony and unanimity of feeling prevailed throughout the day. We

are happy to add that no accident occurred to mar the festivities of the occasion."

It was one of the last news stories Phineas T. Barnum ever wrote. How can a man be content to sit in a dusty newspaper office after a day like that? Four years later, he changed careers:

"In April, 1836, I connected myself with Aaron Turner's travelling circus… We started from Danbury for West Springfield, Massachusetts, April 26, and on the first day, instead of halting to dine, as I expected, Mr. Turner regaled the whole company with three loaves of rye bread and a pound of butter, bought at a farm house at a cost of 50 cents, and, after watering our horses, we went on our way.

"We began our performances in West Springfield, April 28, and as our expected band of music had not arrived from Providence, I made a prefactory speech announcing our disappointment, and our intention to please our patrons, nevertheless. The two Turner boys, sons of the proprietor, rode finely. Joe Pentland, one of the wittiest, best, and most original of clowns, with Vivalla's tricks and other performances in the ring, more than made up for our lack of music. In a day or two, our band arrived and our 'houses' improved.

"While we were at Cabotville, Massachusetts, on going to bed one night, one of my room-mates threw a lighted stump of a cigar into a spit-box filled with sawdust and the result was that at about one o'clock, T.V. Turner, who slept in the

BOSTON

room, awoke in the midst of a dense smoke and barely managed to crawl to a window to open it, and to awaken us in time to save us from suffocation.

"At Lenox, Massachusetts, one Sunday, I attended church as usual, and the preacher denounced our circus and all connected with it as immoral, and was very abusive. Whereupon, when he had read the closing hymn, I walked up the pulpit stairs and handed him a written request signed, 'P.T. Barnum, connected with the circus, June 5, 1836' to be permitted to reply to him. He declined to notice it, and after the benediction, I

Reflected in the mirror-like walls of the John Hancock Tower is Trinity Church **above,** *and* **right** *the golden dome of the Massachusetts State House shines in the winter sun.*

lectured him for not giving me an opportunity to vindicate myself and those with whom I was connected. The affair created considerable excitement and some of the members of the church apologized to me for their clergyman's ill behavior."

Barnum was "connected" with that circus as a ticket-seller and secretary-treasurer. Events like his Lenox lecture were good for business, and good for Barnum, too. Before long, his name was

connected with the very word "circus," and he's still remembered as one of the greatest showmen in American history.

No one but Barnum would have been surprised at the preacher's treatment of the circus, and, obviously, Barnum wasn't really surprised, either. He probably had the note written and the speech prepared long before the preacher wrote his sermon.

Though the early builders of Massachusetts were ready and willing to throw up any kind of a structure, theaters and other places of entertainment were completely out of the question. Even before leaving England, the Puritans had closed down several London theaters. They were a waste of valuable time that could be spent working, in their opinion. And anyone connected with the theater, including Mr. Shakespeare himself, was immoral and indecent.

In 1714, a Boston judge wrote an agitated letter to an associate after hearing that a play was to be performed in his city: "…As much as in me lies," he wrote, "I do forbid it. Let it not be abused with dances or other scenical divertissements. Ovid himself offers invincible arguments against public plays. Let not Christian Boston go beyond heathen Rome in the practice of shameful vanities."

That's not to say Puritan New England was without entertainment. They had sermons on Sundays and every Thursday night they gathered to hear the preacher deliver an uplifting lecture. They didn't celebrate Christmas, but Guy Fawkes Day gave them a chance to let off some steam and say nasty things about Catholics for 24 hours. There were cockfights to go to, and, to make sure the breeding stock of horses stayed up to par, they had a full schedule of horse races. And, although the church strongly disapproved, most people enjoyed dancing. Never on Sunday, of course.

Hymns and other church music were very popular, and it was a natural step from there to staging concerts. But the day-to-day entertainments were simple pleasures by today's standards. A writer in Ridgefield, Connecticut, described it in the 1790s:

"The two great festivals were Thanks-

BOSTON

giving and 'training day', the latter deriving from the still-lingering spirit of the Revolutionary War, a decidedly martial character. The marching of the troops and the discharge of gunpowder, which invariably closed the exercises, were glorious and inspiring mementoes of heroic achievement on many a bloody field. The music of the fife and drum resounded on every side. A match between two rival drummers always drew an admiring crowd, and was in fact one of the great excitements of the day.

"Tavern-haunting, especially in winter when there was little to do, for manufactures had not then sprung up to give profitable occupation during this inclement season, was common, even with respectable farmers. Marriages were celebrated in the evening in the house of the bride, with a general gathering of the neighborhood and usually wound off by dancing. Everybody went, as to a public exhibition, without invitation. Funerals generally drew large processions which proceeded to the grave. Here the minister always made an address, suited to the occasion. If there was anything remarkable in the history of the deceased, it was turned to religious account in the next Sunday's sermon. Singing meetings, to practice church music, were a great resource for the young, in winter. Dances at private houses were common, and drew no reproaches from the sober people present. Balls at taverns were frequented by the young. The children of deacons and ministers attended, though their parents did not. The winter brought sleighing, skating and the usual round of indoor sports. In general, the intercourse of all classes was kindly and considerate ... no one arrogating superiority, and yet no one refusing to acknowledge it where it existed. You would hardly have noticed there was a higher and a lower class. Such there were, certainly, because there must always and everywhere be the strong and the weak, the wise and the foolish, those of superior and those of inferior taste, intellect, manners, appearance and character. But in our society, these existed without being felt as a privilege to one which must give offense to another."

The Puritans kept New England pure

Boston's modern city center soars skyward **left and below left. Above** *the statue of Paul Revere in North End commemorates his famous ride to warn the city's residents of the invading Redcoats.* **Right** *Part of the delightful interior of his house.* **Top right** *is a section of Granary Burying Ground.*

well into the 19th century, and their life style didn't change dramatically until the Industrial Revolution came along to give them "profitable occupation during inclement seasons." As shrewd businessmen, they knew the value of the free energy stored up in those beautiful New England rivers and streams. But once they began building factories and mills, they needed people to provide their energies, too.

The Irish, who were politically oppressed at home, and starving to boot, seemed perfect candidates. And there were others, Germans and Italians, Lithuanians and Poles, Russians and Portuguese all qualified. They'd be glad to emigrate to New England, and happier still to work to help the Yankees earn dollars.

But there was a catch. The labor pool was mainly Catholic. That's what the

Puritans had come here to get away from. Worse, they still had laws that forced people to go to church on Sunday. Not only were they inviting Catholics to invade their sanctuary, but were requiring them to practice their religion in the bargain.

It's a problem that persists to this day.

By the end of the First World War, some 25 per cent of the people living in New England had been born in a foreign country. The parents of even more were foreign-born. Even New York, which loves to consider itself a melting pot, didn't have as many new arrivals as Massachusetts.

The first to arrive were the Irish. Between 1845 and 1850 some 1,500,000 Irish people came to the United States and the majority of them entered through Boston. Another million who stayed behind starved to death. To say they didn't get along with the people who were there ahead of them would be an understatement. The Yankees were still fiercely proud of their British background, and strongly opposed to anything that even hinted at "popery." The Irish, for their part, were just as violently opposed to anything that hinted at anglicism; and they believed that all Protestants were the very opposite of being Christian. The Yankees had already put themselves on the line, more than any other group of Americans, against slavery. They thought women had rights. And they believed that anyone, under the right conditions, of course, could make something of himself.

The Irish Catholics were just the opposite. They believed a man got his

reward in heaven, that a woman's place was in the home and that if all the blacks were free, they'd probably be out of a job.

No two groups ever thrown together had so many differences. Or so much hatred for each other.

The Yankees were first to attack. As the established society, and therefore "the bosses", they set the wages. They were always tight with a dollar, but they set new lows when the Irish arrived. They hired women to work in their homes for $1.50 a week, then kept a third to pay for board. To keep them from doing anything about it, they established special residency laws that kept them from voting. And to keep them "in their place," restricted where they might live. A biographer of the Kennedy family said that when John F. Kennedy's grandfather arrived:

"One sink might serve a house, one privy a neighborhood. Filth spread through courts and alleys, and with it, tuberculosis, cholera and smallpox which thrived in the poorest sections, where the Irish lived."

Only a century before, when the Marquis deLafayette toured Boston, he asked in wonder, "Where are your poor?" Obviously, he got there too soon.

But, as everybody knows, you can't keep the Irish down for long. And their attack was probably as predictable as the Puritans'.

It was only natural they would become politicians, and they became some of the best the country has ever seen. The Yankee businessmen were generally Republicans, and as strong Abolitionists during the Civil War, those on the fence fell on the side of the Grand Old Party. There was no other choice in the Irish neighborhoods than to fall on the other side and become Democrats. They had the advantage of being more numerous as well as more vocal, and, in a democracy that's all the advantage anyone needs. Little by little, they got themselves elected, and little by little began improving things for the people who elected them.

The city's graceful lines are dotted with parks and lakes, and studded with glittering skyscrapers **left.**

THE SPORTING YEAR

But power isn't money. It isn't social position, either. The Yankees controlled New England still. Not as strongly as they had before they were outnumbered, but money and social position were all theirs. As recently as 40 years ago, the "WASP's," as they are called after their Census designation of "White Anglo-Saxon Protestants," controlled the businesses and the banks, the country clubs and important committees; and their neighborhoods were the ones that mattered.

Then one Irishman broke the mold.

He was the grandson of Patrick J Kennedy of County Wexford, Ireland. His father, active in politics, owned a small chain of saloons and was a liquor wholesaler. His name was Joseph P. Kennedy.

His father was the one who broke the mold, actually, by sending him to Harvard.

Bostonians are justly proud of their sporting achievements, with teams like the Red Sox baseball team, championship winners, seen **left,** *and Harvard University football players* **below and right,** *at Harvard Stadium.*

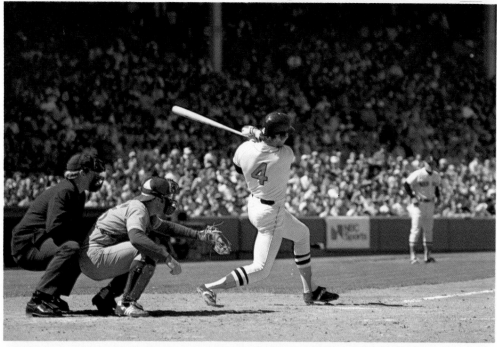

The Catholic Church was officially opposed to Harvard because they felt it opposed them in setting intellectual standards. The result was that very few Irish lads went there. But Joseph Kennedy did, and the old school tie helped establish him as a part of Boston society. When he became president of a small bank, he became a dues-paying member of that society, and it wasn't long before they let him on the Board of Massachusetts Electric, an unheard-of appointment for the grandson of an Irish immigrant.

Twenty years later, after having built a fortune, he was made America's Ambassador to England. After that, differences in New England based on Irish against English background probably seemed silly to a lot of the people involved.

After the end of the Second World War, when veterans were given a free college education, a new generation emerged on both sides of the argument, and more of the old walls came down. But there were more than just two sides to the arguments that were a way of life in the 19th century.

The Irish were first to arrive in the new wave, and were well-established, if not the establishment, when others arrived from such places as Poland and Italy. The old "I was here first" idea that had been used against them became their idea. They dominated the Church and they dominated local politics. And they didn't make life too easy for the other "ethnics" around them. The WASP's, of course, encouraged it. "Let's you and him fight," was their philosophy.

That, too, changed after 1945 when young people came back from the war with fresh ideas, among them marrying as

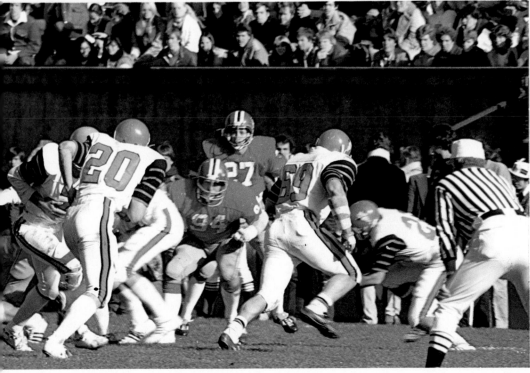

much for love as for ethnic background.

Even though today, more than half of all New Englanders are Catholic, and even though the people there have caught up with the 20th century in their attitudes, the old ethics of the Puritans are almost as important in New England today as ever. And their ideas still dominate all kinds of lives in all parts of the country. They call it "rugged individualism" in a lot of places. Some people blame it on their conscience. It became fashionable when young people started "doing their own thing." And everywhere even cynics admire it as the "American Way". It changes to suit the mood of the country, but the more it changes, the more it stays the same. John Wayne had it; so did the student radicals in the '60s. Labels change, interpretations change. But no other group of Americans had as

much influence on what America is as this group who call themselves New Englanders.

But not all New Englanders are the same. All New England isn't the same. Even within the six states, there are incredible differences. A Maine lobsterman wouldn't trade his awe-inspiring cliffs and the roar of the surf for the life of a potato farmer in Northern Maine. Neither one thinks the high mountains of New Hampshire are nearly as beautiful. And the farmers in Vermont would not dream of trading their quiet green valleys for an obviously infertile place like Cape Cod, no matter how beautiful the Cape is. Cape Codders often run down to Rhode Island, but only to laugh at them for putting tomatoes in the clam chowder. And in the towns along Narragansett Bay, they find it hard to believe that anyone could enjoy life in a place like Connecticut where the sun gets so hot they can grow tobacco. And people in Connecticut couldn't imagine life in the Berkshires where most people haven't got the foggiest idea how to handle a sailboat.

New England is the sea as much as it's the mountains. It's sophisticated cities as much as it is quaint country towns. It's industrial as much as it is farm country. But everywhere you go from Nantucket up to Presque Isle; from the Saint John River down to Candlewood Lake, New England is a thing of beauty.

But it's at its very best in the fall.

Though it has nothing at all to do with a New England autumn, Shakespeare could easily have had such a thing in mind when he wrote these lines about the autumn of life:

> *That time of year thou may'st in me behold*
> *When yellow leaves, or none, or few, do hang*
> *Upon those boughs which shake against the cold,*
> *Bare ruin'd choirs, where late the sweet birds sang.*

Robert Frost, a Californian who spent most of his life in Vermont and New

Hampshire, and captured the spirit of the place almost perfectly, said:

> *The same leaves over and over again!*
> *They fall from giving shade above*
> *To make one texture of faded brown*
> *And fit the earth like a leather glove.*

And Henry David Thoreau, also looking down rather than up, wrote:

> *It is pleasant to walk over the beds of these fresh, crisp and rustling leaves. How beautifully they go to their graves! How gently lay themselves down and turn to mould! Painted of a thousand hues, and fit to make the beds of us living. So they troop to their last resting place, light and frisky.*

It happens every year, the chemistry that lights up the forests of New England touches something wonderful in the human spirit. The chemistry has to do

with a tightening of the cells in the structure of leaves, cutting off the production of chlorophyll and turning them from green to yellow, red, scarlet and hundreds of other colors. The work is done at night when the temperature goes below 45 degrees. It's admired on crisp, sunny days when nothing in the world is better than just being alive.

It starts up in Northern Maine, usually about the middle of September. It spreads south quickly, and most years, all New England is doused in color by the middle of October. The maple, a tree that thrives in all its varieties in all parts of New England, is the most colorful tree in the world, and the only one that turns different colors; some red, some yellow; all indescribably beautiful. Poplars and birches turn lemon yellow; dogwood, mountain ash and barberry turn rich red. Those brownish red trees are probably beeches, and the rich browns are most likely oaks.

Together they add up to a landscape that lures thousands to New England, and New Englanders are ready for them with country fairs and auctions and farm stands brimming with pumpkins and juicy apples, not to mention squashes, corn and gourds. It's the time of year for church suppers and bazaars, arts festivals and just about anything else the natives can think of that will make you want to stay a little longer.

But the tourists who go home with the best memories are the ones who meet nature on her own terms and walk through the woods rather than cruising past them on some turnpike. They're the ones who can tell you what those red berries taste like. Or how it feels to sit on a moss-covered rock under a bright red canopy of leaves and watch a red fox hunting. They can tell you about fields of purple asters that would take your breath away. Or listen to a dog bark miles away and hear no other sound except the buzzing of the bees and the singing of the birds. A flock of geese over a sparkling waterfall, milkweed floss riding on the breeze, a chipmunk racing along the top of a stone wall, are all part of the experience. And on those chilly nights, there is absolutely no such thing as insomnia. The

The vivid colors of fall, and the frothing waters of the many rivers and waterfalls add to the spectacular beauty of New England.

CAPE COD AND THE ISLANDS

mornings, with a dusting of frost on the grass, make you wish the moment would last forever. It's a world of silver and gold, of red and blue, of warm sunshine and cool breezes. But, unfortunately, it doesn't last forever. The "fall foliage" season is only two or three weeks long.

But then the New England winter begins. And there are those who will tell you there's nothing on earth like that, either.

People who prefer winter to fall are probably skiers. The first ski club in the United States was formed in New Hampshire back in 1882, when a very few Americans thought it might be fun to strap some boards on their boots and sail down the side of a mountain. Today, it's almost a national mania, and the most serious skiers in the Northeast find their challenges in the White Mountains of New Hampshire, at Stowe in Vermont, in the Berkshires of Massachusetts or the high mountains of Maine.

The mountains attract almost as many people in the summer, too. Probably the best walking trails in the United States meander through the White Mountains, and probably no one person has ever had the time to explore them all. They come to marvel at Mount Washington, too. When he first saw this highest peak in the Northeast, P.T. Barnum called it "the second greatest on earth." And in spite of a climate up there that can only be described as hostile, there are souvenir stands at the top, and a parking lot. Back in 1934, they recorded a 231-mile-an-hour wind up there that broke every other record that had ever been made anywhere. One year they recorded 569 inches of snow at the summit. And the combination of wind and cold makes it not unusual to feel temperatures as low as 200 degrees below zero on a normal winter day.

But people who make the trip usually say it was worth it, even though Mount Washington is usually covered by clouds. They say watching a sunrise from the summit or seeing the northern lights at night make the wind and the cold almost forgettable.

But of all the unforgettable things about New England, the thing that's probably most outstanding is the seacoast.

CAPE COD AND THE ISLANDS

Although it's only about 250 miles up the coast of Maine as the crow flies, it actually extends for more than 2,400 miles because of all the islands, inlets and bays that were left behind when the glaciers

Cape Cod, and the islands of Martha's Vineyard and Nantucket, offer much to the visitor; charming fishing villages, miles of glorious ocean beaches, every imaginable kind of water sport, historical museums and exhibitions, including a working 18th/19th century farm, and small towns with cobbled streets, steeped in history. Despite the thriving tourist industry, the area remains largely unspoilt, and its character unaltered.

melted thousands of years ago. Those same glaciers gave Maine more than 2,500 lakes, five major rivers and 5,000 smaller ones. They also left behind more boulders than anyone has ever counted.

If you look at a map of Maine, you'll see that the coastline slopes northeastward. But if you talk to a native of Maine, you'll hear they come from "Down East". They're a contrary lot, those New Englanders. But this expression of theirs makes very good sense to them because most of them are sailors. The wind in Maine is mainly (to coin a phrase) from the southwest. To sail eastward, a ship goes with the wind. And, as every sailor knows, that's down.

If you look at a map of Maine, you'll find hundreds of islands along the coast. One of the most beautiful of them, and the most fashionable since back in the 19th century when one of the laws there made you leave your car back on the mainland, is Mount Desert.

CAPE COD AND THE ISLANDS

Mount Desert was once French and was given as a gift to Antoine de la Mothe Cadillac, who later went west to found the city of Detroit. One of the most beautiful spots on the island, Mount Cadillac, was named for him, and not the car.

Bar Harbor is on the island, and has always rivalled Newport as a summer showplace for the super rich. And it also has the first National Park on the Atlantic Coast, a hiker's paradise called Acadia National Park.

Though it's one of the oldest summer resorts in the East, Bar Harbor is surprisingly modern. Back at the end of the 1947 summer season, more than 235 homes and three hotels were destroyed in a fire that European newspapers reported was started by the peasants as a protest against the rich who invaded their town every summer.

Be that as it may, those same "peasants" had a great deal of the town rebuilt for the 1948 season.

They are, after all, Maine Yankees. And there are probably no other people in the world quite like them. The tradition there is to live in small towns. The geography there dictates that even if two towns are no more than five miles apart, you may have to go 25 miles around a bay or an inlet to get from one to the other. As a native Down-easter once explained:

"... Ever since they first came to the Maine coast, they have necessarily been on guard against unexpected attacks from a variety of quarters, including Indians, the weather, the wrath of God, and smooth-talking, out-of-state salesmen. Centuries of defensiveness have trained the Yankee face not to lend itself to merely polite smiles. Such might lead to commitment, and Down-easters have learned not to commit themselves readily.

"An aversion to squandering anything, including time, energy and words is ingrained."

But a disaster like the Bar Harbor fire brings out something else that's ingrained

just as deeply into the Yankee character. They're people you can count on when you need them. They just don't smile a whole lot.

The Maine coast is world-famous, and few seascapes anywhere are as spectacular. But Maine has spectacular forests and mountains, too. It even has a desert. Up near Freeport, a huge area of farmland is covered with sand so deep it covers trees estimated at more than 70 feet high. It just appeared there one day about one hundred years ago and ruined a couple of farms.

The isolation of the Maine coast makes practicing religion a problem. Back in 1905 a couple of Scotsmen solved the problem by starting the Maine Seacoast Missionary Society. According to the story, Angus and Alexander MacDonald were standing at the top of Cadillac Mountain on Mount Desert Island when Alexander said, "Angus, what a parish!" Angus apparently didn't agree because Alexander took it on alone, establishing a small church in a nearby quarryman's boardinghouse. He borrowed some money and bought a sloop he christened "Hope," which he used to reach fishermen otherwise cut off from the Word. Sometimes he was gone for weeks at a time, off in every direction. Before long he bought a bigger boat, called "Sunbeam," and that became the name of the successive boats that carried on the Mission's work, a fleet that eventually led up to cruisers with diesel engines and hulls thick enough to cut through the ice that closes off so many harbors in the winter. They visit lighthouse keepers and lobstermen, fishermen and coastguardsmen who listen to the sermons and join in the hymn-singing.

The biggest event of their year is the month-long Santa Claus cruise when the Sunbeam takes a bit of Christmas to the kids up the coast, out to the lightships, into the small towns where winter has cut the people off from the outside world.

Farther down the coast, the seascape changes and the rocky cliffs are replaced by the high sand dunes of Cape Cod. The Cape has more than 40 miles of the most beautiful sandy beaches anywhere on the East Coast. And anyone who has ever

Fishing is still a major industry along the coast of New England, and the area's restaurants are rightly famous for their sea-food specialties.

CAPE COD AND THE ISLANDS

driven over the Cape Cod Canal to hit a solid line of traffic can attest to the fact that tourism is the Cape's biggest industry.

That hasn't always been the case. Back in the days of the hard-working Puritans, it had a huge commercial salt works, plenty of farms and fishing villages and a ship building industry as big as any in New England. Glass was made there, and so was rum. The Puritans never found any great pleasure in surfing.

The original flavor of the place has been preserved in the Cape Cod National Seashore, which protects the beaches and salt marshes from any more man-made interference.

Cape Cod is also the jumping-off place for two of the most beautiful spots in New England, or anywhere else: Nantucket and Martha's Vineyard. The Vineyard, they say, was first discovered by Leif Erickson and his Norsemen, who were impressed by the number of grape vines growing there and called it "Vinland The Good." Naturally, the Norsemen didn't write anything down, and the place was lost to history until an English ship landed there in 1602. The grape vines impressed them, too, but even more, they were pleased, after a long sea voyage, to find "divers sorts of shellfish, as scollops, muscles, cockles, lobsters, crabs and wilks, exceeding good and very great."

They sat down and had New England's first shore dinner. And while they were there, they probably had the first clambake, too. It's an institution we should all be grateful for. By tradition, the New England clambake must be prepared on the beach. That's where the shellfish are freshest, the air clearest and the sounds and smells the greatest. It begins with a pit in the sand that's filled with rocks and driftwood. By burning the driftwood for a couple of hours, the rocks get very hot and ready to be covered with damp seaweed. Fresh clams are spread over it along with potatoes and onions, fish and possibly some chicken. After that, lobsters and corn. The whole thing is covered with an old piece of sailcloth and then everybody goes to play in the surf for an hour to work up an appetite. When they get back, all that good food is ready to be eaten with melted butter and gallons of

cold beer. You can usually spot the tourists in the crowd because they use knives and forks.

And there are plenty of tourists to spot at Martha's Vineyard during the summer. The normal population of the island is something less than 5,000. Something like ten times that number live there in July and August.

About 40 miles away, and 30 miles out to sea, Nantucket is like a place that time forgot. Back in 1672, a Nantucketer spotted a whale swimming offshore and had an idea. It was the same idea those London businessmen had hoped would inspire Captain John Smith a century before. Whales were a good cash crop back then, and Nantucket an ideal spot to

Dating back to 1630 is the windmill **far right** *built by the Plymouth Colony around the area of Eastham, although Penniman House* **below left** *was built more than 200 years later. The historic town of Sandwich, near Cape Cod Canal, features beautiful old weathered buildings* **left and below.**

go out after them. The place boomed. It wasn't long before there weren't any whales off Nantucket any more, but they had good ships and went all over the world to hunt them down.

It lasted 100 years. During that time, Nantucket was the third most important city in New England, taking a back seat

only to Salem and Boston. It had a population of more than 10,000 and a whaling fleet of about 100 ships. It was easily the most important whaling port in the world. Then the bottom fell out. Demand dropped for whale oil, and the city was nearly destroyed in a fire in 1846. With that, most of the residents went back to the mainland and left behind a town that didn't have any factories, or slums, and no reason for new immigrants to come. The result is that Nantucket today is an almost perfectly-preserved 19th century New England town. Oh, there are mopeds on the streets and an occasional French restaurant, but the sense of history on Nantucket is stronger than almost any place in the United States.

The whalers were rich, and their mansions were meant to impress their neighbors with that fact. They impress visitors today. Across the island, in the tiny town of Siasconsett, other seafaring people built homes of a different kind. They were fishermen from Portugal who built tiny cottages on the high dunes and planted climbing rose-bushes around them, as if to provide anchors to keep them from blowing away. The cottages are smaller and less impressive than the whalers' mansions, but they were after smaller fish, after all.

Siasconsett was for years a haven for actors and others in the entertainment business, and the main street in town, not much more than a narrow lane, is called "Broadway."

CAPE COD AND THE ISLANDS

Between the two towns the island is a broad expanse of moors, complete with thistle and heather. The only difference between it and the moors of Scotland is an occasional cranberry bog. Though New England is not quite like any other place in the world, most travellers agree it's more like Scotland than anything.

Why then, you might ask, was the

Overlooking the surrounding waters is the Sankaty Head Lighthouse **below,** *on the island of Nantucket, while Mill Creek Marsh* **right,** *is set in the little town of Sandwich, Cape Cod. The clear pond* **far right** *framed by burnished forest land, is part of the 2,000 acres of state park, established in memory of Roland C. Nickerson.*

territory north of it called Nova Scotia? After having given New England to the Puritan interests, King James I decided it was a good idea to keep them from expanding all the way to the North Pole (as they surely would have done!). To accomplish it, he gave the territory along the Bay of Fundy between the ocean and the St. Lawrence River to a Scottish crony. It seemed unimportant to him that the French had already claimed it, and even had settlers living there. But he named it Nova Scotia, and if emigrants from Scotland were a long time coming, the name stuck.

No matter where New Englanders came from, they're marked in the rest of the United States by their accents. To anyone but another New Englander, the speech patterns in Boston and the conversation of a State-of-Mainer are both the same. Up north in Maine and New Hampshire, the accent is probably closest to the original Yankee dialect. And the farmers will tell you that farming there would be better if there weren't so many "stuns" in the field. They drop the "r's" from the ends of words in Massachusetts, and the "a" sound in the middle of words gets broadened so a park is a "pahk." In Connecticut and some parts of Vermont, the same word is "parhk." And in Western New England, the "r" that's dropped by easterners is picked up and even emphasized.

The farther south you go in New England, the more likely you are to run into people who aren't New Englanders at all, but people transplanted from other parts of the country. Connecticut, especi-

ally, prides itself on being "corporate headquarters" for dozens of companies that moved up from New York in search of lower taxes and easier living.

Many a Connecticut farmer has sold huge chunks of meadowland to companies like I.B.M., taken the money and run south to Florida. The companies then replace the meadows with asphalt parking lots and dot the hillsides with aluminum and glass boxes they call office buildings. They cover the whole thing up with

nursery-grown trees and conduct their business in splendid isolation. It's the wave of the future, they'll tell you, to decentralize outside the big cities. No matter that it's also outside human contact and the people who work in the glass boxes are virtual prisoners there.

They do have one big advantage. They get to live in New England.

Henry David Thoreau summed up what it means to be a New Englander:

"No people can long continue provincial in character who have the propensity for politics and whittling, and rapid traveling, which the Yankees have, and who are leaving the mother country behind in the variety of their notions and inventions. The possession and exercise of practical talent merely are a sure and rapid means of intellectual culture and independence."

And the newcomers usually become New Englanders quickly because it's an infectious way of life. They buy houses

built along the same lines as the ones the early settlers built because, like so many other things about New England, the design is practical.

If they work in glass boxes, they live in salt-boxes. It's a steep-roofed house based on the homes the Puritans left behind in England. They were usually two stories high with one room and a vestibule on each floor. As the settlers became more prosperous, they modernized by adding a second room on each floor but, essentially, they just built a second identical house up against the existing one. As their families grew, they added one-story extensions to the back of the house and brought the roof line down to cover it. The overall impression was that of a salt box, and that's where the name comes from.

The houses were always built around a huge fieldstone fireplace, sometimes as much as 12-feet-square. Oak timbers were cut by hand and wooden pins were made to hold them together. When it came time to raise the center beam and construct the frame, everyone in town came to help. After the party was over, a man was well on his way to having his house finished; all he needed to do was close it in with cedar shingles and finish the inside room.

Though construction isn't as much fun these days, the basic salt-box design is more common in New England housing developments than more modern split levels or ranch houses. And that helps New England keep some of its character in spite of a new invasion of immigrants.

New England farmers are likely to have second jobs in factories these days, and new industries are springing up all over the place. Newcomers are moving in on the bankers. And prosperity seems to be the word of the day. But as much as outsiders are changing Yankee attitudes, one old idea that's been there since the beginning has become New England's greatest export.

It's called knowledge.

During World War II scientists became the country's elite. And New England, particularly at Harvard and the Massachusetts Institute of Technology, had the country's greatest concentration of scientific knowledge. Yale, Brandeis,

Bass Harbor Lighthouse **top left** *is pictured dramatically silhouetted against the setting sun, while* **below left** *the kissing bridge at Blair on the Beebe River stands against an autumnal sky. This page: these monuments honor* **top** *John Harvard, and* **above** *the Mayflower Pilgrims.*

The University of Connecticut and others made New England the center of higher education in the country. Today those institutions are still leading the way in research and development, and that has attracted electronics and aerospace companies. Scientists like New England because it's a pleasant place to work. And as long as they feel that way, that's good for New England.

It is a pleasant place to live and work. It's contemporary, but it's traditional, too.

It's a place where a quiet country town with a white church steeple exists comfortably next to an industrial complex with a grey water tower. It's a place where pride still lives. Where people care about each other and make visitors feel welcome. It's six of the smallest states with the heaviest concentration of population. More important, it's a state of mind. It has a rich history and a bright future and people with a good sense of what both can mean.

And is the future bright? How can it be otherwise from the place that gave the country such things as Christian Science and M.I.T., hand-made quilts and machine-made cotton, the Farmer's Almanac and Fannie Farmer? It's the land of P. T. Barnum and the Kennedys, of Howard Johnson and the Harvard Business School. Its legacy includes Ted Williams and Carl Yastrzemsky, Rocky Marciano and the Boston Strangler. It gave us Lizzie Borden and the Salem witches, public schools and fire insurance. Where would we all be without cranberry sauce or clam chowder, beach plum jelly or Maine potatoes? And what about maple syrup, baked beans, codfish or Boston lettuce? L. L. Bean is an institution we all appreciate, so's the Boston Symphony and the Red Sox. New England gave us WASPs and R. H. Macy, Jimmy Foxx and Joe Cronin, the Brinks robbers and whalebone corsets. Bayberry candles light up our holidays, nutmegs add spice, sou'westers keep us dry, Narragansett Beer wets our whistle.

New Englanders gave us codfish and quahogs and atomic submarines. They gave us the Americas Cup Races and Waltham watches, town meetings and mill towns, village greens and fall colors. Kids blame New England for public schools, but did you ever meet a kid who didn't enjoy a lobster dinner?

The list is endless, obviously, and it includes such delights as scrimshaw and hard rock maple, Arthur Fiedler, Tanglewood, Newport jazz and Gloucester fishermen. But their most important contribution is what makes all the others work. It's called Yankee ingenuity. Without it, New England would probably still be part of the British Empire and New York would still be Dutch.

First English edition published in 1981 by Colour International Ltd.
This editions is published by Crescent Books, Distribuited by Crown Publishers Inc.
Illustrations and text ©: Colour Library International Ltd. 163 East 64 th Street, New York 10021.
Colour separations by FERCROM, Barcelona, Spain.
Display and text filmsetting by Focus Photoset, London, England.
Printed by Grafiques Excelsior S.A. Bound by Eurobinder, Barcelona, España.
Library of Congress Catalog Card Number: 81-67582.
CRESCENT 1981.